Diary
of a
Pioneer Boy

Written by Elizabeth Massie

Illustrated by Domenick D'Andrea

STECK-VAUGHN
ELEMENTARY · SECONDARY · ADULT · LIBRARY

A Harcourt Classroom Education Company

www.steck-vaughn.com

Contents

CHAPTER 1

Moving to Montana

April 28, 1885

Dear Diary,

My name is Ben Wilkins. I live in St. Louis, Missouri. I will not live here for much longer, though. We are moving! My mother got me this little book and some pencils so I could write about our move and our new life.

Last night I lay awake in my bed. My mother and father were in the kitchen. I could hear them talking to each other.

"I can no longer make a good living in this city. It's time to go west," my father said to my mother.

My heart began to flutter. My older brother, Conrad, whispered, "Father wants us to move!"

"Andrew," said my mother, "I know it has been hard to find work lately. I think you are right. It would be good for us to make a new start."

"Yes," said Father, "it is time to move on. More families have moved here. Many of the men are carpenters, too. Soon I will be out of work."

I think my parents knew we could hear them because they began to whisper. The only thing I heard them say after that was "Montana."

My older brother, Conrad, grumbled into his pillow. My sister, Sarah, came in from her room. "I don't want to leave here," she said. "I don't want to leave my friends!" Gabriel, the baby, made a little crying sound in his crib.

Montana. I don't know much about it, but I like the sound of it. My sister and older brother don't want to leave St. Louis, but I do. I want to go somewhere I've never been. I want to be an explorer. I want an adventure!

4

On June 2, 1885, Ben Wilkins and his family loaded their new wagon with mattresses, tools, chairs, and trunks. They had sold their home on Bryant Street. They had also sold most of their furniture to their neighbors. Their wagon, like those of other pioneers, did not hold much.

Ben's father told him to load the blankets and pillows. "Let your brother handle the heavy things," he said. "We don't want anything broken."

At last they hitched their two horses to the wagon. Ben's father tied the children's pony, Scout, to the back of it.

As the Wilkins family pulled away, Ben waved good-bye to St. Louis. He waved to the shops, to the trolley cars, and to the gaslights. He was happy to be leaving. Ben's journey had begun.

June 8, 1885

Dear Diary,

For six long days we have ridden down winding roads and along a big river. We sleep in the wagon every night. We eat biscuits, dried beef, and cheese for every meal. I wish I could have some fresh tomatoes and some bread with butter.

Conrad and Father went hunting for squirrels this morning, but Father wouldn't let me go. My mother told me I could go hunting when I was older. "You are too young," she said.

I do not like being treated like a baby. I am not very strong, but I am smart and quick. Someday they will see. I will show them!

The Wilkins family arrived in Independence, Missouri, on June 10. There they joined four other families who were also traveling west. Traveling together made the long trip safer for everyone.

Before the families left Independence, they bought supplies to last them on their journey. There were few stores on the frontier. Ben's father bought a cow so that his children would have milk. Ben's mother stocked up on flour, corn meal, salt pork, and potatoes.

Traveling with others meant that Ben had other children to play with. He became friends with a red-haired boy named Joshua, who was a year younger.

Whenever they had a spare minute and a creek nearby, the two boys headed off to fish. Ben learned to catch catfish and perch, but he still dreamed of going hunting. Joshua's father often took Joshua hunting with him at dusk. Ben watched with envy as Joshua brought back rabbits and groundhogs to have for supper.

"Father, I know I would be good at hunting," Ben told his father every night.

Ben's father just laughed and said, "Someday, son. Right now I've got Conrad to help me do the hunting."

Sarah's job was to take care of little Gabriel while their mother cooked meals and washed the family's clothes. For three months Ben spent almost every evening helping his mother. She taught him how to clean the fish he caught. She taught him how to cook them over an open fire. She even showed him how to clean the pan with sand.

CHAPTER 2

Losing Scout

September 6, 1885

Dear Diary,

After fourteen weeks in the wagon, we have finally arrived in Montana. Father bought some land to build a ranch and raise cattle. He and Conrad built a small barn for the animals and a little lean-to for us. Now every day we work on our cabin and our fall garden. Winter comes early in Montana, so we must finish the cabin soon.

Our valley has very few trees. It is mostly grass and brush. The pine trees for the barn and the cabin come from the foot of the mountains to the south. Father and Conrad chop them and haul them back with the horses. Then my father cuts notches at the ends of the logs. The notches make the logs fit together at the corners of the cabin.

In truth, Conrad, Sarah, Mother, and Father are building the cabin. I am sent to do chores that a four-year-old could do. I have to mix mud and grass. Then I must help Mother and Sarah stuff it between the logs so that rain and snow won't blow in the cabin.

St. Louis seems very far away now. Sometimes I miss our house on Bryant Street. I had lots of friends to play with. Joshua and his family went on to settle in Oregon. I haven't made any friends yet in Montana. No other children live close to us.

September 8, 1885

Dear Diary,

Mother and Sarah have finished planting cabbage and kale in our garden. They have tied bits of tin on strings to keep the birds away. I must do more chores. Today my job is to water the baby plants and hoe weeds. When I get time, I like to sit down and write about all the new things I have seen in Montana.

Father and Conrad left early this morning. They are going into town to buy supplies and several head of cattle. They will be the first of my father's herd of beef cattle. Father has heard that other families in Montana have become rich raising cattle.

11

Two mornings later Ben found himself attached to the hoe again. He slammed the hoe into the dirt and grumbled to himself about his aching back. Then something his mother said made Ben's ears perk up. She was telling Sarah that she needed some new baskets to gather the vegetables they would have in late October. She said the reeds growing by the creek were good for weaving.

Ben was tired of hoeing weeds in the garden. He wanted to ride Scout to the creek to get the reeds. He wanted some adventure.

"I'll go!" Ben called to his mother. "Give me the sack, and I will collect the best reeds ever!"

Mother shook her head. "No, I think Sarah should go. I must have good, strong reeds. Sarah is older and will be careful to get the right kind."

"I can be careful," Ben replied. "I'm not a little boy anymore."

Sarah was standing on the bench outside the cabin door. "Let him go, Mother," she urged. "He always fusses that he has to do baby chores."

Mother held Gabriel and patted him on the back. She looked at Ben thoughtfully. "You will be careful and come right back?" she asked.

"I will. You don't have to worry," Ben replied.

With a slight frown, she nodded at last. That was all Ben needed. He dropped the hoe in the middle of the garden. He saddled Scout, grabbed the sack, and was off.

September 10, 1885

Dear Diary,

   I am in trouble, and I do not know what to do. Here is what happened. This morning mother sent me to the creek to get reeds for her. At first I was happy. I was out by myself, and I wasn't hoeing weeds or mixing mud.

   I rode Scout north along the creek, pulling reeds here and there. We chased rabbits, and I found some snake holes along the creek bank. I didn't get too close to them, though. They were big, and I figured that the snakes that made them had to be big, too.

   I was so busy having fun that I didn't notice the day had grown misty and cool. The clouds covered the sun. I could no longer tell which way was south. At first I thought it didn't matter. I could find our cabin by following the creek.

   I climbed back onto Scout. At that moment one of the creek snakes slithered by Scout's foot. Scout took off in a gallop.

"Whoa!" I yelled. I pulled back on the reins as hard as I could. But Scout was panicked. He wanted to get as far away from that snake as he could. On he raced into the misty fog that was settling close to the ground. We reached a gully, and Scout leaped over it. I fell off and hit the dirt.

My head hurt. "Scout, come back!" I yelled.

The sound of his hoofbeats disappeared in the fog. He was gone.

"Scout!" I yelled again. There was no sign of him. I knew then that I was truly lost.

I walked for a long time. I called for Scout, and I looked for the creek. I must have walked for miles. I wished I had a stick in case a wildcat came along. We saw many coyotes, foxes, and wildcats on our journey from St. Louis, but I was always in the wagon, and my family was always with me.

And now I am sitting by a large boulder, hoping the fog goes away soon. It is hard to see much except these words. I must be brave. I told my mother I would come right back. I told her I would be careful.

A noise!

CHAPTER 3

A Noise in the Fog

When Ben heard the strange noise near him, he crouched low against the boulder. He listened to the odd sound, his heart beating wildly.

Rattle-rattle, growl! Rattle-rattle-grunt, growl! Never had Ben heard such a noise. He held his breath and trembled like a leaf in the wind. The sound got closer and closer. RATTLE-RATTLE, GROWL! RATTLE-RATTLE-GRUNT, GROWL!

Ben covered his eyes, hoping whatever it was would go away and not see him. Then he heard a cough. And a sneeze. And another growl. The thing was just on the other side of the boulder. Very slowly Ben raised his head enough to peek out. There in the fog stood a rickety wagon with a driver wearing several layers of clothing.

"Hello, there!" called the driver in a growling, scratchy voice. "I can see you, don't think I can't!"

Dear Diary,

It turned out that the noise was someone in a wagon. The person was so bundled up that I thought I was looking at a scarecrow. I ducked down and held still. The scarecrow climbed down from the wagon. "What are you doing out here all alone?" I heard it ask.

Suddenly a big hand grabbed my collar and yanked me up. A big, round face pushed right into mine. I stared. I blinked. It wasn't a scarecrow after all. It was a woman as old as Grandmother Wilkins back in St. Louis. She had cracked lips, dark skin, and wrinkles across her cheeks. She wore a man's big jacket and trousers. Her hat was pulled down so low that I could hardly see her eyes.

"Who are you, boy? What are you doing here?" demanded the woman. "Were you waiting to jump out and steal my mares from me?"

I was so shocked that I couldn't answer the woman. She thought I was a horse thief!

Then the woman leaned back, put her hands on her hips, and began to laugh. She laughed and laughed.

I didn't laugh. I frowned.

She stopped laughing and said, "I know you are not a horse thief. No! I think you are a boy who has gotten himself lost. Are you lost, little boy?"

I told her I wasn't a little boy and I wasn't lost.

"Oh?" she asked. "All right, then. My name is Mary Fields."

She asked me if I wanted to stay with her until the fog lifted. I said yes. I really didn't have any choice.

CHAPTER 4

Eyes in the Darkness

"Mary Fields, that's me," said the woman to Ben as she struck a match on the bottom of her boot. Then she leaned over and lit the pile of sagebrush she'd collected. "I've been driving the road to St. Peter's Mission for many a year. Want some jerky?"

Ben told her no and sat down near the fire.

"Might as well take some," Mary said. "A lost boy—if there was a lost boy anywhere around here—gets pretty hungry. Besides, neither one of us is going anywhere for a while."

Ben didn't answer. But after a moment, he took the jerky.

"You a pioneer?" asked Mary around a big wad of jerky. "You and your family just move to Montana?"

"I'm an explorer," Ben answered. "I've been looking for gold." It was not the truth, but Ben didn't want Mary to think he was just a child.

"Indeed? And where did you live before you came here?" she asked.

"St. Louis," he said. "Missouri."

"Find any gold yet?"

"Not yet," he told her.

"It's hard to look for gold without a horse, pick, or shovel," Mary observed.

"I have a horse, only he's lost," Ben said.

"I see," Mary replied, nodding slowly.

Dear Diary,

The woman and I sat in the fog and waited for it to lift. She lit a fire and made coffee. Then we talked for a while. Her name is Mary Fields. She says she was born in 1832 on the Dunn family farm in Tennessee. Mary was friends with Dolly Dunn, but Dolly moved away when she grew up. When the War Between the States was over, Mary left the Dunns.

"I found some work," Mary told me, "but something inside me said to go west and find adventure!"

"Adventure?" I asked her. "That's why I came here, too."

Mary rubbed her chin. "Yes, adventure. I came to Montana and took to driving a wagon. I move things from where they are to where they have to go."

Mary goes back and forth between town and the mission. She picks up tools, books, and medicine in town and takes them to the mission. Mary was on her way there when the fog rolled in.

"There's nothing better than living under a big sky, with fresh air, freedom, and adventure," she said.

"What kind of adventures do you have?" I asked. But at that very moment, Mary Fields jumped to her feet in her big, old boots and held out her hand to me. "Shhhhh!" she whispered. "I reckon we've got ourselves an adventure right here!"

I jumped up, too. Mary looked deep into the fog. I looked deep into the fog, too. At first I couldn't see anything except gray mist. Then I saw them—big yellow eyes all around us on all sides, watching us. Out of the mist stepped a pack of huge timber wolves.

I was about to scream. Mary slapped her hand over my mouth. "Shhh!" she said. "An explorer like you should know how to handle a few wolves."

"Handle wolves?" I whispered, my heart beating like a rabbit's. "People can't handle wolves!"

Mary gave me a sharp look. "Do what I do," she told me. She put her hands on her hips, leaned forward, and opened her eyes wide. Her eyebrows formed a tight line, and her mouth made a snarl. "Get back, you rascals!" she snapped.

I leaned forward and stared just like Mary. Slowly the wolves pulled back and disappeared into the fog. Mary patted me on the back and said, "I call that making wolf eyes. It scares them away every time!"

Mary plopped back down on the ground and took a drink of water from her canteen. I drank some, too, when my hands had stopped shaking.

The Long, Rocky Road

"You can make a lot of friends out here in the wilderness," Mary told me. "Elk, beavers, birds, even wolves sometimes. I never get lonely."

I noticed that the fog had begun to fade away. Before long I could see clearly all around. But I still did not know where I was.

Mary stood up. She kicked dirt on the fire to put it out and said, "It's getting late. I'll be going my way now, and you'll be going your way. Good-bye, young explorer!" Then she got quiet and looked at me. I could tell she was waiting for me to say something. I said I would be heading home and told her good-bye. I didn't want her to know I was lost.

As Mary Fields's wagon rattled away through the grass, Ben looked north and south, east and west. He knew he could not find his way home. "Come back!" he shouted.

Mary pulled the horses to a stop and looked over her shoulder at Ben with a smile. "What?"

"I don't know how to get home," he blurted out. "Will you help me?"

Mary rubbed her chin. "Yes, I'll take you home. But first you'll have to ride with me to St. Peter's Mission. I'm late already."

Dear Diary,

I am now beside Mary on the wagon. We are rolling along a bumpy trail. It is late afternoon, and I know my family must be very worried about me. I don't want to go any farther from home, but I have no choice. I don't know where home is.

We've reached the foot of the mountains and are climbing through trees and rocks. I can hardly write because the ride is so rough.

Bear!

Dear Diary,

It's finally safe to write again. When the bear began to follow us, I tugged hard on Mary's sleeve. "Look!" I said.

Mary looked back. "That old beggar! Smells my jerky, he does, the old busybody!"

The bear was snorting and trotting along just yards behind us. He looked very hungry. I wasn't going to wait for him to jump in the wagon. I hopped in the back, picked up two of Mary's pans, and smacked them together. The bear stopped in his tracks. I smacked the pans again. He grunted and waddled off.

Mary slapped her knee and grinned at me. "Good job, young explorer! I couldn't have done better myself!"

I climbed back to my seat, feeling very proud of myself. The trail became steeper. The horses had to work hard to pull the wagon up the rocky road. Mary talked to them. "Come on, girls. You can do it! You can do it!"

At the top of a ridge, Mary pulled the horses to a stop. She sniffed the air, then quickly drove the wagon behind some thick spruce trees. She got down to hold the horses still. I didn't know what was wrong.

For the first time since I met her, Mary looked worried. Then I heard the horses' hooves and the men's voices.

"Outlaws!" Mary whispered to me.

I knew about outlaws. They stole gold and horses. They were bad men. What if they saw us? What if they heard us?

The men stopped their horses on the other side of the trees. One man got down to stretch his legs. He looked all around as he walked. Then he said, "I heard something, Bill! Did you? Let's check on the other side of these trees." The other outlaw slid down off his horse.

Mary looked frightened. I grabbed a hammer from the wagon and threw it as far as I could. It landed with a crash in some weeds.

"It's probably just a critter over there in the brush," said the man. "Let's get down the mountain while there's still some daylight."

Mary smiled a big smile. When the men were gone, she looked at me and winked. "Was that enough adventure for you?" she asked.

I said it was more than enough.

CHAPTER 6

The Mission

It was night by the time Ben and Mary reached St. Peter's Mission. Ben could see light sparkling in windows as Mary drove closer. The mission was like a fort, with a wall all around and lots of buildings inside. When Mary reached the gate, she shouted, "Mary is here with the goods!"

The gate opened with a loud creak. Once Ben and Mary were inside the walls, Mary jumped down and hugged the woman who had opened the gate. It was hard for Ben to see the woman's face, but her voice sounded kind. "Welcome home, Mary!" she said. "I hope your trip was safe."

"For the most part," replied Mary as Ben hopped down beside her. "This young explorer helped me along the way. He's mighty handy and mighty smart."

The woman shook Ben's hand. "I am Sister Amadeus," she told Ben. "Pleased to meet you."

"Do you remember the Dolly Dunn that I told you about?" Mary asked Ben.

Ben nodded.

"Sister Amadeus is Dolly Dunn," said Mary. "We grew up together in Tennessee. Now we're together again!"

Dear Diary,

We finally reached the mission after dark. Several women and children came out to help unload the supplies. I helped, too. They didn't tell me to carry the little things like Father does.

Later we all sat down to supper in a building they call the main hall. Mary and I ate with the children, the women, and some men who helped out. We had potatoes, chicken, beans, and berry pie. Food had never tasted so good in all my life.

Now I've written down all I can remember about today's adventures. The happy talk and the good food make me think of home. I miss my family. I am tired.

When Ben woke up the next morning, the sun was bright. He was lying on a cot, and he had a pillow under his head. But he was not at home. He was still at the mission. He slid off the cot and ran outside.

Mary was talking to the women about repairs that the roof of the main hall needed. Ben decided to look around. Outside the front gate he found a pasture with goats. Inside the wall, he found a chapel and a paddock with sheep, pigs, and a black pony. There was also a hospital. Ben went inside quietly.

CHAPTER 7

Home Again

September 11, 1885

Dear Diary,

I explored the mission this morning. The last place I went was a white building. I think it is the hospital.

"Hello," a small voice said from a cot in the corner. It was a girl. She looked very sick. I said hello to her and told her my name. She said her name was Suzanne.

I wondered how I could make Suzanne feel better. I decided to sit with her and draw a picture. Then I showed her how to write her name. She tried hard, but her letters came out crooked. She laughed at how funny they looked. I gave her a pencil to keep.

When Mary called me, I told Suzanne good-bye. Outside the hospital, a woman told me that it might be a long time before Suzanne would be well. That made me sad.

Mary and I waved good-bye to the people of St. Peter's Mission. We drove out across the field toward the hills. We were but a short distance away when we heard a shout. Sister Amadeus was running after us, leading a black pony. "Wait!" she called out to me. "This is for you!" I didn't understand what Sister Amadeus meant.

"The pony belongs to Suzanne," Sister Amadeus explained. "Her name is Tess. But Suzanne cannot ride now. She wants you to have Tess. She insists that you take her."

At first all I could think of was having a pony all my own. No more sharing Scout with Conrad and Sarah. What adventures Tess and I could have!

Then I noticed that Mary and Sister Amadeus were studying me. I thought about Suzanne and the right thing to do. "Tell Suzanne I will take care of Tess for her, but Tess is still hers. I'll have Tess waiting for her to ride when she gets well."

Mary and I drove the horses for hours, back across the mountains and down to the grassy plains. The black pony pranced behind us. I told Mary about the creek that went by my cabin and how it twisted and turned.

"Ah, yes," she said. "I know that creek. We will find it, and we will find your home!"

It was late in the afternoon when I saw the roof of our little cabin and the fence around our garden. I jumped from Mary's wagon and ran all the way to the door. My mother met me and hugged me so hard I could hardly breathe. "Ben!" she cried. "Where in the world have you been? We've been worried sick about you!"

"So it's Ben, is it, young explorer?" asked Mary, who had pulled up beside the cabin.

My father hugged me, and Sarah and Conrad, too. Then my mother frowned. "I knew I shouldn't have let you go for reeds! You are too young for dangerous chores!"

"Oh, I don't know about that," said Mary. "Ben is quite a young man! He helped me stare down wolves, chase away a bear, and trick outlaws! I couldn't have made it to St. Peter's Mission without this young man."

"Indeed?" asked my mother.

"Indeed?" asked my father.

"Indeed!" said Mary with a laugh. "And he has a fine, true heart." She told them about Suzanne and the pony.

My mother and father thanked Mary for her kindness. After we all bid her farewell, I showed my family Suzanne's pony. Then I remembered Scout. Scout was still missing. Poor Scout!

My father smiled at me. "Will there be room in the barn for two ponies?" he asked me. I ran to the barn, and there was Scout in his stall, munching hay. He had found his way home before I did!

At bedtime, my father told me he knew I was not a little boy anymore.

I am lots of things. I am grown up. I am a pioneer. I am an explorer. But best of all, at least for now, I am home.

The End